LIMITLESS EMPOWERMENT

Dear Danni,

You are limitless!
I wish you all the
success in the world!
Dream big!

Love
Anika x

LIMITLESS EMPOWERMENT

UNLOCKING YOUR INFINITE POTENTIAL

15 NO NONSENSE WAYS TO

STEP INTO YOUR POWER
TAKE BACK CONTROL
& BELIEVE IN YOURSELF

ANIKA PATEL

Cover design by Anika Patel
Book design & Content Creation by Anika Patel

ISBN: 9798313352732

Dedication

Dedicated to everyone that has a big imagination. I empower you to keep dreaming big, take that chance and go for everything that you want in life and turn those dreams into a reality, as anything is possible. You are worth everything that you desire!

I also dedicate this book to all the people who have taken that step and jumped out of their comfort zone and have followed their passions in life and made a success out of it. This has inspired me to follow my dreams and love of writing too.

Table Of Contents

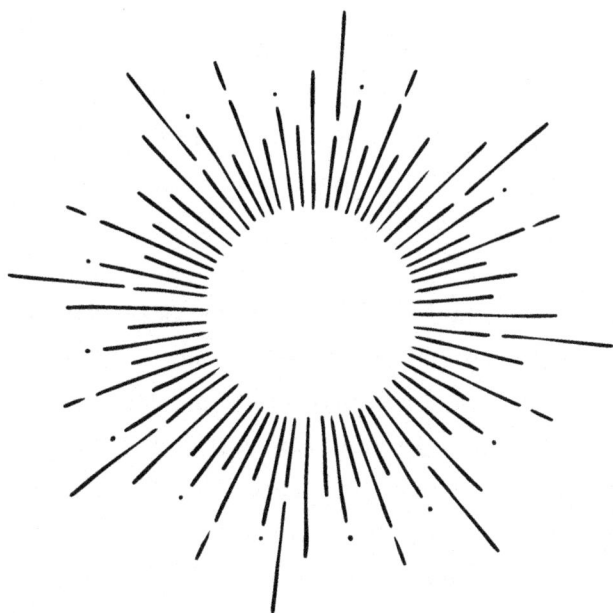

Acknowledgements

I want to thank my supportive and loving partner, my family and friends who have encouraged, supported and believed in me to write this book.

I also want to thank my social media communities for the daily support on my 'Empowering the Mind' page. The love, encouragement and kind words are truly amazing, and it encourages me to keep writing and sharing my voice and journey daily to empower everyone to love themselves from the core, realise their worth and limitless potential, and be the best versions of themselves.

Introduction

Did you know that many of us spend a lifetime trying to gain that self-confidence to really believe in ourselves, yet this is the key component that affects almost everything in life, and especially our happiness and success?

There is a certain type of freedom that comes when you let go of limiting beliefs and start to empower yourself, and once you get to that point, there is no going back. Our life really begins when we start to put ourselves first and choose our happiness over anything else. It all starts by taking care of YOU!

I am still on that self-love and empowerment journey. It is a lifelong commitment, and I am continuously doing the inner work. Becoming self-aware is really inspiring.

This is the second part of my 'Committed To Me' mini book series, following on from self-love. This book is committed to help you to realise your worth and limitless potential.

I have written this mini-series to express:

- The importance of committing to building a relationship with yourself.
- The importance of working on your personal

development for your mind, body and soul.

- The importance of how to stop leading with fear and learn to love yourself unconditionally from the core and unlock that limitless potential and confidence that we all have within us.

When I think about having limitless empowerment, I think of prioritising self-care, self-love and being kind to myself, by how I speak and think about myself. I think about stepping into my power, taking back control, and believing in myself. It could mean saying NO and setting a boundary, it could be saying daily affirmations to boost self-esteem or meditating to feel balanced and grounded. But, how do we get to that state of mind where we can feel so empowered daily?

It takes a lot of inner work and daily self-improvement habits, which eventually become a part of your lifestyle. It means letting go of thoughts and patterns that no longer serve us and reprogramming our subconscious minds and years of conditioning. It means really looking at who you are and healing past wounds and completely accepting yourself. It's like pressing the refresh and restart button on your life, but it is worth it!

I believe that making this investment in yourself is so important, it is the best investment that you will ever make.

So, I would like to take you through the different ways that you can work on yourself to feel empowered, confident, and realise your worth.

In this short book, I go through my favourite self-worth and empowerment quotes, which I expand on and share my knowledge and experiences with you on what being self-empowered and having limitless potential means to me, so that you can have an insight into how to believe in yourself from the core.

I really hope that by sharing my journey and voice, I can inspire, encourage and motivate you to also commit to yourself or continue this journey if you are already on it.

So, who is with me?

Self-acceptance is the key to limitless empowerment…

Dear reader,

I want you to know that you have the power to empower yourself, you are worthy and good enough to do whatever you desire in life...And most importantly, you have the potential to achieve your dreams.

I want you to believe in yourself.

I want you to go for what you want in life and fulfil your dreams because you CAN! And, if anyone tells you that you can't, don't listen. Trust yourself and the journey that you are on, as everything is unfolding in your favour.

66

'NO ONE CAN MAKE YOU
FEEL INFERIOR WITHOUT
YOUR CONSENT'

Eleanor Roosevelt

Chapter 1

I do not give you permission to define me...

...Because I know who I am!

'You're so ugly'
'You are a loser'
'You're so fat'
'You don't know anything'
'You are so stupid and dumb'
'You're so dark'
'No one will marry you if you look like that'
'You are not naturally beautiful like your cousins'
'My complexion is better than yours'
'You need to dress for your age'

These are just a few of the things that I was told growing up by various members of my extended family, along with the dirty looks, smirks, being laughed at and made fun of, ALL OF THE TIME at family get togethers.

No wonder I thought there was always something wrong with me. As I got older, I noticed similar patterns like the above, which I experienced at school, college, university and even in the workplace.
I felt like I never really fit in with any groups and that I did not have real friends growing up. In my 20's this was hard,

as I really wanted to be included and have friends to socialise with, so I ignored the comments, looks and being spoken about behind my back and stayed in situations which were not really for my highest good. I know, shame on me!

I wanted to be included. I wanted to be invited to that party or be a part of that 'girls trip'. I was working overtime to be liked and 'fit in' with people who, quite frankly, when I look back, were adding nothing to my life.

I know! What was I doing?!?

I guess I didn't want to be rejected or feel alone. But there is nothing more lonely than being surrounded by people that you cannot be yourself with or trust. I eventually let these people go along the way. I wanted to be surrounded by people who were for me, not against me, as that makes the world of difference. With that, comes a lot of courage, strength...AND BOUNDARIES.

People came and went as the years went by, I was starting to tolerate less and learnt that I'd rather be alone than be continuously disrespected and unhappy.
I was finally learning boundaries (but, I still had a long way to go).

The key word here being, SELF-RESPECT.

And, also realising that I no longer give people the power or permission to tell me who I am because I started to gain the confidence to define and know who I was becoming. I no longer needed or wanted validation from anyone, as I realised that me validating myself was enough. As long as you are not hurting or disrespecting anyone, including yourself. GIVE YOURSELF PERMISSION TO BE YOU...And remember that you will never be everyone's cup of tea, and that is OK.

People will always talk, let them. We cannot live our lives based on the opinions of others, otherwise you will lose yourself completely. I have to remind myself of this sometimes, as I do tend to let it get to me at times as well.

So, remember that the only validation that you need is from YOURSELF!
The only persons opinion that really matters is your own.
If you let someone else create the narrative of your life, you will only begin to become resentful.
The power is in your hands. You must believe in yourself so much that nothing can shake you.

BECOME UNSHAKABLE!

During my healing journey, I experienced the loneliest time. It is what I like to call the 'shedding phase', because as I started to heal the wounded parts of myself and gained more of an understanding, I was growing and evolving, which led to me letting go and walking away from friendships, family members, and people that brought me down. It is a very uneasy and awkward phase of life, but eventually the right people will come to you as you start to align with the best and new version of you. So, make room for them and say bon voyage to the rest!

During this time, I learnt to sit alone, in my loneliness and started to embrace it and became my own best friend. I started to enjoy my own company. I became brave and so self-empowered that I didn't need people around me anymore to be happy.

I love 'me time', whether it is going to the cinema alone, sitting in a café having brunch, exploring in a museum and even solo travel. It is true bliss when you reach that point.

I no longer want to fit in.

I no longer care about being included.

I no longer wait for that invite.

I no longer crave that friendship or company.

My circle may be smaller, but so much more supportive and positive.

I no longer let anyone's words make me feel inferior or less than.

I no longer allow people to create my narrative.

I no longer let people tell me who I am. Why should they?

I embrace every part of me and know that I am enough...
And so are you.

I want you to build that confidence and self-assurance to the point where you know that you are going to be fine with or without anyone – STAND IN THAT POWER!

Be your authentic self and allow the right people that will serve your highest good to come to you.

BECAUSE WE DON'T CHASE – WE ATTRACT!

When we set that boundary, we are telling ourselves that we deserve to be treated better!

66

'BELIEVE IN YOURSELF'

Unknown

_____

Chapter 2

Fancy placing a bet on yourself...

Did you know that when you believe in yourself, you are unstoppable!

Did you know that when you believe in yourself, anything is possible?

Did you know that believing in yourself is one of the secrets to success?

Believe in yourself so much that you know that you will always be able to bet on yourself, and win!

Know that you have the self-confidence, determination and limitless potential to go after what you desire and whether it works out or not, you have given it your 100% effort.
It starts with you! The first person that you should believe in is you! Have faith and know your capabilities. This belief helps you overcome self-doubt and gives you the confidence to take action.

We all have dreams, but how many of us really take action to achieve them?
A dream written down with a date becomes a goal. A goal broken down into steps becomes a plan.

A plan backed up by action makes your dreams come true. So, make your dreams a reality. If I can do it, so can you. You just need to take that step!

Try these 5 ways to start believing in yourself by:
- Being your own coach and first point of contact to resolve any issues.
- Focus on your strengths
- Embrace who you are!
- Get comfortable with being uncomfortable
- Believe that you can!

I didn't always believe in myself because a lot of people around me didn't believe in me and that did not help my confidence and self-esteem. I didn't believe in myself enough to go for high paid roles or senior positions, even though I could do the job. I always used to see myself as inferior to others. I didn't feel important or valued in my friendships either.

I wanted this to change as I felt that I also deserve a fulfilled life. But in order to do this, I needed to start with myself and change my mindset, my belief system and the narrative that I had about myself. Your mindset shapes your life and I needed to turn my thoughts about myself around.

Being surrounded by positive and supportive people really helps with feeling confident and empowered. Sometimes it can take just one person to believe in you and give you that push and confidence to kick start your journey in believing in yourself.

It helps you to take risks. For example, with me, I started writing my books and set up my online businesses so that I could design my dream life.
When you start to jump out of your comfort zone, pushing boundaries and taking those steps, you feel empowered to go for what you desire.

As I have also taken those steps, I am able to share my journey and experiences with all of you, in the hope that I can inspire you to do the same.

I just wanted you to know that I believe in you!

I know that you are capable of anything that you want to do!

I know that you have limitless potential.

I know that you can do anything that you put your mind to!

66

'YOUR SELF-WORTH IS NOT BASED ON THE OPINIONS OF OTHERS'

Anika Patel

_____

Chapter 3

The only validation that you need is from YOURSELF!

Relying on someone to tell you who you are is like handing over your life and putting it in their hands to play with.
We need to instill so much confidence within ourselves, so that we can define ourselves without letting others do it for us!

Have enough confidence to know that you are worthy, enough, important, smart and intelligent without needing reassurance from anyone else.
No one can tell me who I am... when I know who I am first!

This takes daily practice as there are going to be people and external factors that try to bring you down! But stay strong.

If you are not sure of yourself, how can you expect someone else to have faith and confidence in you and what you bring to the table.

If we live our lives wanting to be accepted by others, we will not be able to survive their rejection. Living this way will not serve our highest good!

The key is self-confidence!

A lot of us spend years criticising ourselves and that leads to more negative feelings and self-doubt. I have done it too. But why not try and see what happens when you start to approve of yourself and affirm positive words about yourself too. Your mindset will start to shift, and you will feel more empowered to seize each day!

Be kind to yourself. It will give you the confidence that you need to be happy and content. Not needing that approval from people will set your mind and soul free.

I say this because for years I was trapped internally in my own mind. I filled it with negative self-talk, self-doubt and never felt good enough. It stems from other deep routed trauma and experiences, but I secretly wanted to be validated by everyone around me...BUT WHY?

I never felt good enough. You couldn't see this on the outside, but deep down the little girl inside me wanted that validation from her mother, her father, her family. Who doesn't? It takes a lot of strength to get to a place where you don't care about what your own parents think of you.

The traumatic effect of invalidation left me feeling worthless, inadequate, not enough and not having much sense of self, with a side helping of shame and guilt. I never felt seen, heard or understood. I didn't feel important to them either. I started to dismiss myself and my feelings.

I do remember my grandma and close aunty giving me that daily love and re-assurance as a young child, but I was not always with them.

Who you spend the most time growing up with can really shape who you become as you grow up.

It was only in my mid 30's that I started to gain a better understanding of the harm this has done to myself and my life. That's when I started my healing journey so that I could give myself a chance to live a better life, and most importantly, be happy.

Because, why am I not important?

Why should my feelings not matter?

Why should I not be seen or heard?

Think about that. I'd like you to write down what you feel when you read those questions.

I want to share these three unique approaches to build self-confidence and self-empowerment that go beyond conventional advice with you:

1. Build "Radical Self-Awareness" by Embracing Your Inner Contradictions

Why it's unique: We often think of confidence as having a consistent, flawless image of who we are and what we want. But real self-empowerment comes from embracing the full spectrum of who you are, your contradictions, vulnerabilities, and strengths.

How it works: Instead of trying to be perfect or fit into one specific role, acknowledge that you can be multifaceted. Maybe you're both introverted and extroverted, or you're a perfectionist and someone who enjoys imperfection. Accepting these contradictions allows you to feel empowered in your complexity, giving you the freedom to act confidently even when you don't fit a neat, "ideal" mold.

Action: Write down two or three contradictions within yourself (e.g. "I love solitude, but I also crave connection") and let yourself sit with these contradictions without trying to resolve them. This will help you feel whole, rather than divided.

2. Master the Art of "Self-Referencing" (Stop Seeking Validation from Others)

Why it's unique: Traditional advice often says you should stop seeking validation from others, but what if the real secret is to become your primary source of validation? The power of self-referencing comes from consistently looking inward rather than outward for approval or confidence.

How it works: Instead of waiting for someone to praise your achievements, trust your own inner feelings. Every decision, big or small, should be checked against your values, not someone else's expectations. When you build your sense of worth on your own terms, you feel self-empowered even when the outside world is silent or indifferent.

Action: Next time you're about to make a decision, ask yourself, "Does this align with my true self?" By checking in with your own values first, you'll build a more authentic sense of confidence.

3. Leverage "Purposeful Vulnerability" to Unlock Your Strengths

Why it's unique: Most confidence advice focuses on strength, but true empowerment often comes from being vulnerably honest about your weaknesses, and using them as sources of power.

How it works: Rather than hiding your vulnerabilities or trying to seem invulnerable, lean into them. Vulnerability isn't about weakness, it's a way to connect with others and learn more about yourself. Embracing your insecurities or fears allows you to see them not as obstacles but as tools for personal growth. This can shift how you show up in the world, making you feel more confident because you're no longer hiding parts of yourself.

Action: Pick one area where you usually feel insecure and share it with someone you trust. Observe how embracing this vulnerability transforms how you interact with others and, most importantly, with yourself.

These strategies encourage a deeper, more detailed understanding of confidence and empowerment, moving beyond the typical "fake it 'til you make it" advice to something that feels more genuine and sustainable. Which one resonates with you the most? For me it is embracing my inner contradictions like practicing gratitude, meditating and manifesting, yet also being a worrier.

And remember this…A woman who does not require validation from anyone else is the most feared individual on the planet! How powerful is that!

Affirm it daily!

"

'CONFIDENCE IS SHOWING
UP IN EVERY SINGLE
MOMENT LIKE YOU ARE
MEANT TO BE THERE'

Unknown

Chapter 4

The power of believing in yourself...

One of the greatest challenges I have faced on the journey to self-empowerment is overcoming the doubt that has clouded my potential. The world may seem full of obstacles, opinions, and criticisms, but none of them are as paralysing as the doubts that I have held about myself. Believing in myself was the first step to unlocking the power that I had within me, and it's not just a momentary thought, it's a mindset, and a way of life. I still have moments of self-doubt. We all do, but it is how we overcome these fears. Are we going to let it consume us and do nothing or are we going to build our self-worth and confidence each day and keep going.

I sometimes wake up and think, what am I doing? Can I succeed in my ventures? Will I be able to write another book? Then I stop and give myself a virtual slap and a pat on the back as I know that my determination will get me to places.

If you are feeling that you cannot believe in yourself. Let me help you!

Understand The Power Of Belief

Belief is the foundation of all action. Think about it, before you can take any steps to achieve your goals, you first have to believe that those goals are attainable. Without belief, there is no motivation to try, and without effort, there is no result. When you believe in yourself, you send a powerful message to the universe that you're ready to receive the success and fulfilment that you deserve. Belief in yourself doesn't just magically appear, it takes practice, nurturing, and growth. It's not about being perfect or having all the answers, it's about trusting your ability to figure things out as you go. Visualise it. You will feel better! Create a vision board, they help you feel so much better on low days. I look at mine daily.

Shift Your Mindset

Make it bullet proof. The way you think about yourself directly impacts how you act. Negative thoughts like "I'm not good enough," "I'll never succeed," or "I don't deserve happiness" only serve to reinforce feelings of inadequacy. But these thoughts are just that, thoughts, not facts. The key to shifting your mindset is to catch these negative thoughts and challenge them. When a thought like "I'm not good enough" arises, counter it with "I am capable of learning and growing." When you believe in your potential, you begin to see opportunities instead of obstacles and solutions instead of problems.

A powerful technique for transforming negative self-talk is affirmations. These are positive, present-tense statements you say to yourself to reinforce your self-worth. For example:
- "I am worthy of love and success."
- "I am enough, just as I am."
- "Every day, I get stronger and more confident."

By repeating these affirmations regularly, you start to change your internal dialogue. Over time, these positive thoughts become your reality. I did this every single day for a year and still do. It helped me shift my mindset and gain self-belief and confidence when others around me were trying to bring me down.

Build Confidence Through Small Wins
Confidence is built through experience, and experience comes from taking action. One of the best ways to start building belief in yourself is by setting and achieving small, manageable goals. These wins, no matter how minor they may seem, serve as proof that you are capable. Each small success fuels the next, and the momentum will grow.

Start with something simple that you can do today, whether it's making a phone call, completing a task at work, or setting aside time for self-care. As you accomplish these small goals, you'll start to see evidence of your strength and ability. With each step, your belief in yourself will become more grounded.

Embrace Failure As a Stepping Stone

It's important to remember that self-belief isn't about avoiding failure, it's about learning how to handle it with grace and resilience. Failure isn't a sign that you're not good enough. It's a lesson in how to improve and grow.

When you fail at something, instead of berating yourself, ask yourself what you can learn from the experience. What went wrong? What can you do differently next time? This mindset shifts failure from being a setback to being an opportunity for growth.

Remember, even the most successful people in the world have faced failure. What sets them apart isn't their perfection, but their ability to bounce back and keep going. If you don't give up, neither will your belief in yourself. So please don't be embarrassed of any failures. It is a part of life and what makes you...YOU! I have failed many times, but I see it as a learning curve. I would rather try and fail than not try at all.

Trust Yourself on This Journey

Believing in yourself is not a destination, but a continuous journey. It's about recognising your inherent worth, embracing your imperfections, and committing to your own growth. When you believe in yourself, you unlock the door to endless possibilities.

After all, believing in yourself is the first secret to success.

"

'MAKE PEACE WITH
YOUR BROKEN PIECES'

Unknown

———————————————————

Chapter 5

Let the light shine in!...

Affirm it! 'I make peace with my broken pieces'

Acceptance is the key word here. This is important if you want to make changes in your life. Becoming self-aware of yourself is the first step.

When we are self-aware, we can learn more. We are also open to new opportunities and possibilities, and the ability to change and grow. No one is perfect. We all have our flaws, weaknesses, insecurities, wounds and triggers. It is about getting to a place where you are willing to face these parts of you and do the inner work. Start with small steps.

So, how do we move on from the pain of our past? I find that expressing my pain is helpful. However, there is a balance between wallowing in self-pity and the negative feelings (as that is not healthy either) or trying to avoid the feelings altogether. I find journaling useful and writing how I am feeling and what I am grateful for. It can be a great way to release negative feelings from your mind and body. Talking to someone that you can trust is also helpful and takes a weight of your shoulders.

It is important to acknowledge the role that you have played in this too and take responsibility without blaming yourself too much either. All these experiences can either shape who you become and teach you valuable lessons or consume you and your life.

It is a long and painful process, but take your time, and if it gets too much then take a break and focus on the present moment and affirm what you are grateful for. Take a walk, go to the gym, listen to some music, read a book or watch your favourite tv show. Embrace your surroundings, it will help with the healing journey.

It is ok to ask for help from friends, family or a professional. Remember that healing is your own sacred journey, and each person will have their own way of doing it, with the right support and guidance. Be mindful of who you also confide in as not everyone may understand the journey that you are on and that is ok too.

When we start to let go of the past, we can accept and embrace our future. I know that it can be a difficult thing to do especially if we have regrets and wish that we had done things differently. But we cannot live in our memories. I am guilty of this too. I have regrets that I did not spend enough time with my close aunty that passed away. There were circumstantial reasons behind this and yes, I could have done more, but I did as much as I could.

I forgive myself for this as it is a crucial part of moving on. I have learned from this and will do better in the future.

Here are a few affirmations to stay present when you find yourself deep in regret or overthinking about things that are no longer in your control:

'At this moment, I feel thankful for my purpose in life'

'I welcome my feelings without judgement'

'My life is always in the now'

'I live fully in this moment and embrace my future'

'I am more aware and alive at every moment'

'I let go of the past'

'I am in control of myself'

"

'ACCEPT YOURSELF.
THEN OTHERS WILL TOO'

Unknown

Chapter 6

Self-confidence is my best outfit!

Well…I am still working on that. I have my moments of feeling less than I actually am.

I sometimes still let others' opinions of me and their comments consume me, but I am only human. I often wonder if I will ever be enough for myself, my friends, my family…even my partner.
What I seem to forget as I ride this rollercoaster called life, is that I hold the power.

I know that I am enough. I used to always worry if I would meet someone that would also realise that and see my value and accept me as I am. Accept my strengths, weaknesses, perfections, imperfections, flaws, beauty and so on. Luckily, my partner has embraced every part of me, and I have also in return done the same.

When we fully accept ourselves just as we are and are also willing to work on the parts that we need to improve on, we learn to let go of certain expectations and pressures that we put on ourselves and just let it be.

That is the start of becoming self-empowered.

You cannot force anyone to see your value. It will consume you and you will lose yourself in the process. You will not need to convince the right people to see your worth. And this goes for people in the workplace too as well as your friendship circle.

People assume, judge, make presumptions and that's fine! – LET THEM.

If they want to misunderstand you without actually getting to know you – LET THEM

Stand in your power so much that it does not bother you – WHY SHOULD IT?

The right people will accept all the parts of your being and encourage you to evolve and grow into the best version of you. Be fussy with who YOU want around you. Not who you want to be around. When you think like this, your confidence in yourself will increase and your anxiety will start to reduce.

It takes time, and we will have our ups and downs with this. I still do. But, when I remember who I am and how far I have come and what I have learnt along the way, I feel better knowing that I am doing the best that I can, for myself.

The journey of self-acceptance and embracing who you are can feel like an uphill battle. In a world where external expectations dictate how we should look, feel and behave, it can feel overwhelming.

So...What Is Self-Acceptance?

Self-acceptance, to me means embracing every part of yourself, even the parts that aren't perfect. It means acknowledging your strengths and flaws, your victories and mistakes, and recognising that they all make you who you are. It's about letting go of the need for approval from others and understanding that your worth isn't based on anyone's standards but your own.

Self-acceptance means that we will eventually let go and stop needing that approval from external factors around us.

The Struggle With Self-Acceptance

For many of us, the journey to self-acceptance is filled with challenges. Society often pushes unrealistic standards, whether it's about appearance, success, or relationships. We compare ourselves to others and judge ourselves harshly when we don't measure up. This constant pressure can make us feel inadequate, but it's essential to remember that no one has a perfect life, and everyone is on their own path.

Here are 4 reasons why self-acceptance is crucial:

1. Improves Mental Health

Accepting who you are reduces stress, anxiety, and negative self-talk. When we stop trying to be someone that we're not, we can find true inner peace.

2. Encourages Growth

When you accept yourself, you acknowledge that you're not perfect. This acceptance opens the door for growth because you can identify areas you want to improve without feeling like you're a failure.

3. Boosts Confidence

Self-acceptance is the foundation of confidence. The more you embrace your unique qualities, the more confident you'll become in expressing who you are.

4. Strengthens Relationships

When you're at peace with yourself, your relationships with others improve. You can be authentic without fear of judgment or rejection.

7 Ways to practice self-acceptance

1. Stop Comparing Yourself to Others

Social media and society often set unrealistic benchmarks for beauty, success, and happiness. Recognise that your journey is yours alone. Focus on your own progress instead of comparing it to others.

2. Be Kind to Yourself

Practice self-compassion. Talk to yourself the way you would talk to a friend who's struggling. Be gentle and understanding, not harsh and judgmental.

3. Celebrate Your Wins

Big or small, celebrate your achievements. Recognise your progress and be proud of yourself for overcoming challenges.

4. Let Go of Perfection

No one is perfect, and neither are you. Instead of aiming for perfection, aim for growth. Accept that making mistakes is part of the learning process.

5. Surround Yourself with Positive People

The people you spend time with can influence how you feel about yourself. Surround yourself with individuals who lift you up, support your dreams, and appreciate you for who you are.

6. Reflect on Your Values

Identify the things that matter most to you. Align your actions with your values and let that be your guide, not the opinions of others.

7. Practice Gratitude

Gratitude shifts your focus from what you don't have, to

what you do. By appreciating your unique qualities and life experiences, you'll start to see how amazing you really are.

Self-acceptance is a journey, not a destination. It requires time, patience, and practice. But every step you take towards accepting yourself is a step towards greater peace and happiness. Remember, you are enough just as you are.

So, embrace your imperfections, celebrate your uniqueness, and know that you deserve all the love and respect you give to others. The more you accept yourself, the more others will too, and ultimately, the more fulfilling your life will become.

If you're ready to begin your journey towards self-acceptance, take it one day at a time, and be kind to yourself along the way.

And remember…You are enough. You always have been.

"

'DUST SETTLES.
PEOPLE SHOULDN'T'

Unknown

_____

Chapter 7

Know your worth and add tax!...

There came a time in my life when I gained the confidence to know my worth and add that tax! And I am glad that I did, because I am worth it! And so are you!

It meant that I was not afraid to lose people anymore or walk away from that job or relationship.
When you have a pure soul and a kind loyal heart, you do not lose people. They lose you.

When you understand yourself and know what you bring to the table, you are not afraid to walk away from what no longer serves you.

When you know that you deserve to be treated with respect, you realise that you should not be settling.

But why do we settle? It is due to fear.
Fear of not feeling worthy or good enough. Fear of thinking that we should not dream big and doubting ourself. Fear of starting again. Fear of making a mistake. Fear of our age. Fear of thinking that we cannot do better. Fear of being alone. Fear of not having the right skills. The list is endless but it is the main factor. Well, it was for me. This is why I used to settle.

When we let go of that fear and step into our power, the game changes because we have finally realised our worth. Knowing that gives us limitless potential.

I will be honest. I used to settle. I did not believe that I deserved the best in life, in relationships, and in the jobs that I wanted. It left me unhappy because I had the potential to do better but I was holding myself back!

One day I decided that enough is enough, because I wanted a better life for myself, a good career, a loving partner and a meaningful life. The power was in my hands to make that change. I needed to recognise that I am worthy by setting boundaries, saying no, to stop making excuses and instead, make a plan of action to change my old habits…because Anika, my dear, you were never meant to settle.

Once I realised this, I decided to make changes in my life, starting with the people that I surrounded myself with. I let a lot of them go. I wanted to be around positive, kind people that were supportive.

I started to make a plan for the life that I wanted and I decided to do much better when it also came to the partner that I desired and would want by my side.

Only we can make the decision to change our life. It is worth the risk, regardless of the outcome. The first step is to realise that you want better. The rest falls into place.

Why have a mediocre life when you can have an extraordinary one!

"

'SHE REMEMBERED WHO SHE WAS
&
THE GAME CHANGED'

Lala deliah

_____

Chapter 8

I am back! Are you ready!...

Insecurities are loud. Confidence is silent.

We all go through ups and downs in life. It is all a part of it. But we must make sure that our comeback game is so much stronger, for no one, but ourselves!
You have nothing to prove to others, just to yourself.
When you remember who you are, the world better watch out because there is nothing more intimidating than someone who has risen from the dirt that he or she was left in! I hope that has given you some excitement and confidence for the day!

I remember this so clearly. It was October 2019. I was in my hotel room in Bristol, unable to get out of bed, staring into nothingness. I had no idea how to help myself, but I had hope. I asked for a miracle. I knew that I needed to face myself and my pain and walk through it, to start living a life beyond my wildest dreams.

The first step is acknowledging that something is wrong.
The second, is to want to do something about it.

Emotional rock bottom is where I realised that the only way is up. I remembered one of my favourite sayings, that the wound is where the light enters.

There must be a reason behind this pain, these experiences and these lessons, but are we willing to really learn and find out why?

The healing journey can be a hard, painful and lonely place, but those who choose to walk down that path of transformation can not only help themselves, but help others too. I decided to help others through my books and share my experiences and journey to help others in similar situations. Healing is not linear. There will be days when you want to give up and take steps back and that is ok. Keep pushing forward. It will be worth it.

Healing is on-going. It takes a lifetime to unlearn old habits and improve ourselves for the better, but with that can come compassion, understanding and self-awareness.

After nearly 3 years of working on myself, I started to find my purpose and understand myself better. I had a better understanding of the experiences that I went through and what is was teaching me. I started to let go of anger, hurt, guilt, shame and resentment, and learnt to accept that this is and was my journey to learn hard lessons, embrace them and be a better version of myself.

I was learning boundaries, having a voice, saying no without worrying what the outcome would result in. I felt much more confident and worthy. I stopped settling.

I remembered that I deserve the best in life and that is what I will wait for.

I turned my pain into my power, and I will continue to light the way for others.

Remember who you are before the world told you who you should be!

66

'YOU ARE NEVER TOO OLD TO
SET ANOTHER GOAL AND LIVE
THE LIFE OF YOUR DREAMS'

Anika Patel

Chapter 9

Age is just a number...

It is never too late to start something new in life. Break free from age limits. It is all in your mind.

It is a common belief that we all hold, but dreams don't have an expiry date.

Look at certain famous food chain owners. They didn't find success until their 60's. Their persistence paid off and it created global brands.

A lot of fashion designers became renowned in their 40s. This is the same for chef's and actors as well. True fame arrived later in their life.

There is no right time to pursue your dreams. There is no age limit either. So, just start. Waiting or holding yourself back will only lead to regret. Fear of worrying that it may not work out will only leave you powerless. Wouldn't you rather try and fail, than not try at all?

What is failing anyway? And why are we so afraid of it? I see failing as an opportunity to learn lessons so that I can do better next time.

If we don't fail, then we won't grow. Would you rather stay where you are than move forward?

Being 'too old' is just a myth and by believing in this, you are missing out on success, adventure and fulfilment.

When we pursue our dreams, it can be enriching no matter when it happens. You become wiser and knowledgeable. And knowledge is power!

Yes, we all have our setbacks. I have had many too, but I have reframed them into powerful lessons that have provided me with resilience and a clear perspective to move forward.

Use your setbacks as a vital part of your story that enhances the dreams that you are working towards, instead of thinking of them as barriers.

It is never too late to start out. If you are feeling discouraged or stuck, it is important to remember that you can reinvent yourself at any age.

To do this, there is a level of self-confidence and self-belief that is required, as we know that there are going to be people that are not supportive, and fill us with self-doubt, including ourselves. Push through these feelings and do it

anyway. I want to share a few tips on how I overcame my
fear of living my dream life.

I identified my true passion
I often felt stuck because I was not clear on what I truly
wanted. I reflected on what excited me, what I was
naturally good at, and what would make me feel fulfilled. I
started self-discovery through journaling, meditation, or
simply asking thought-provoking questions like:

- What did I love doing as a child?
- What brings me joy, even in small doses?
- What would I do if money and time weren't an issue?

When you understand your true passion, it becomes easier
to take the first step towards your dreams.

I changed my narrative around fear
Fear often held me back from pursuing my dreams. It could
be fear of failure, fear of judgment, or fear of the unknown.
I empower you to reframe fear as a sign of growth and
transformation. Fear is not something to avoid but
something to embrace. It's a natural part of stepping outside
comfort zones. Take small, manageable risks and look at
failure as a stepping stone to success.

I built a growth mindset
I encourage you all to develop a growth mindset. Abilities

and intelligence can be developed through dedication and hard work. Setbacks or mistakes are just opportunities for learning. With this mindset, you will be more resilient in the face of challenges and more open to new experiences. You can start by:

- Focusing on progress rather than perfection.
- Learn from every situation.
- Research stories of others who succeeded after multiple failures.

I set achievable goals and broke them down

Having a clear vision is powerful, but without action, it remains a dream. Set specific, measurable, and achievable goals. Break these goals down into smaller, actionable steps so you don't feel overwhelmed. As you start to accomplish each step, you will build momentum and gain confidence.

Example: My dream was to write a book. I was terrified. In fact, I kept putting it off and wanted to give up numerous times. However, I set aside time each day to write for 20 minutes, and later, broke down the process into outlining, drafting, and editing phases. Micro tasks help with productivity and efficiency.

I ensured that I stayed consistent

Empowerment often comes from ongoing support. Start to build habits that lead to long-term success, whether it's dedicating time to your dreams daily or surrounding yourself with positive influences. Celebrate small wins along the way to keep your motivation high.

I encourage you to:
- Stay consistent, even on tough days.
- Surround yourself with people who inspire and uplift you.
- Reflect on your progress regularly.

I practiced self-compassion

Sometimes, self-doubt can stop someone from pursuing their dreams. I encourage you to have self-compassion. Treat yourself with kindness and understanding when things don't go as planned. This mindset allows you to bounce back quicker from disappointments and keep going.
- Speak kindly to yourself
- You don't need to be perfect to be successful.
- Focus on your strengths instead of weaknesses.

I embodied resilience and self-belief

I would say I am an example of resilience and self-belief. I have had many setbacks throughout my life. However, I have always known that living my dream life is possible and that setbacks don't define my ability to succeed.

I shifted my perspective

I saw challenges as opportunities. Shift your perspective on challenges. Life's hurdles are often the catalysts for personal growth. When I have been faced with obstacles, each one has provided a lesson or a new opportunity. I embrace challenges as part of the journey rather than seeing them as roadblocks.

Example: If you face rejection, it might be a chance to refine your approach or learn something new about yourself.

I gave myself permission to dream big

Sometimes people hold back on their dreams because they feel undeserving or are afraid that they will fail. I empower you by giving you permission to dream big. Your dreams are valid, no matter how audacious they might seem. In fact, it's often the boldest dreams that lead to the most fulfilling lives.

I encourage you to:
- Dream without limitations.
- Visualise your ideal life as already happening.
- Take steps towards those dreams, no matter how small.

I practiced gratitude

Gratitude is a powerful tool for empowerment. By focusing on what you already have, you can shift from scarcity thinking to abundance thinking. Gratitude helps to attract more of the positive energy that you need to pursue your dreams.
- Practice gratitude daily
- Notice the small blessings that align with your dreams.
I want you to know that you can achieve your wildest dreams, regardless of when you decide to start.
You have the power to unlock your potential.

Your dream life is waiting for you, not in 10 years' time, but NOW.

The power to shape it is in your hands. Don't regret it!

66

'THE MOST COURAGEOUS
ACT IS STILL TO THINK
FOR YOURSELF. ALOUD'

Coco Chanel

_____

Chapter 10

The courage to think for yourself and speak out loud...

One of the most powerful acts of self-empowerment is the courage to think for yourself, even when it challenges the status quo. Our world is full of expectations, societal norms, family expectations, workplace standards, that often discourage independent thought and self-expression. To break free from this cycle, you must have the courage to think for yourself and speak your truth, even if it means standing alone. I have always spoken my mind and vocalised my thoughts. If I am not hurting or disrespecting anyone including myself, why should I be scared to speak out. In Indian culture, women have always been expected to be seen and not heard, but that has changed a lot over the years.

From a young age, I was conditioned to conform to follow rules, agree with the majority, and prioritise the opinions of others over my own. But when we silence our own thoughts and ideas to fit in, we lose a part of our authenticity. Independent thinking is about reclaiming your voice and trusting your own intellect and intuition, regardless of what others think or expect.

The courage to think for yourself can be seen as an act of rebellion against the pressure to blend in. It required me to have confidence in my perspective, even if it was different or unpopular. By thinking independently, you create space for fresh ideas, solutions, and new possibilities. You give yourself permission to be original, to take risks, and to break away from conventional paths. I never really fit in with the norm. I used to think that I was a bit different from my friends, family and colleagues, but that was because they were not my circle of like-minded people at that time. I eventually found my circle. If you don't fit in around the table, then create your own and don't be afraid to do it!

The most common barrier to speaking out loud and thinking for yourself is the fear of judgment. I used to worry about what others would think of me, whether they'll accept or reject my ideas, or if I would be misunderstood. This fear kept me from speaking my mind and following my own path.

But here's the truth, judgment is inevitable. No matter how carefully I used to phrase my thoughts or how much I tried to fit in, someone, somewhere, always had something to say. The only question is whether you'll let that fear control you or whether you'll choose to live authentically. You are not going to be everyone's cup of tea...and that is ok.

You cannot please everyone...and that is ok, too!

I tell myself, not everyone will like my book and what I stand for…but that is fine because I will find the people who do enjoy it and that will be my audience.

I am not going to let that fear stop me.

That leads me to my next point, self-trust is the foundation of thinking for yourself. When you don't trust your own ideas or judgments, you'll constantly seek validation from others. This dependence on external approval keeps you stuck in a cycle of doubt and hesitation. Building self-trust involves practicing confidence in your decisions and thoughts. You don't need to have all the answers, but you do need to trust that your perspective is valuable. The more I started to trust myself, the more I felt empowered to speak out loud, even when my ideas felt bold or unconventional.

Remember, every time you speak your mind, you're not only standing up for yourself, but also setting a precedent for others to do the same. Self-trust builds your confidence and reinforces your belief in your ability to navigate challenges and uncertainties.

When you think for yourself, you will undoubtedly encounter disagreement. Not everyone will agree with your ideas, and that's okay. True empowerment comes from knowing that it's possible to disagree without losing your sense of self-worth or feeling invalidated.

Disagreement is not a sign of failure, it's simply a reflection of diverse perspectives. Instead of retreating in the face of disagreement, embrace it as an opportunity for growth and conversation. Respectful disagreements can lead to deeper understanding and can help you refine your ideas.

The goal is not to convince everyone to agree with you, but to create space for open dialogue where all voices are heard and valued.

To think for yourself and speak your mind is an act of vulnerability. You are putting your thoughts, your beliefs, and your identity on display, and that can feel intimidating. But vulnerability is not a weakness, it is a strength.

When you allow yourself to be vulnerable, you open the door to deeper connection with others. You give others permission to do the same. Vulnerability leads to authenticity, and it is through authentic self-expression that you create meaningful relationships and impact.

Don't be afraid to express yourself, even if it feels uncomfortable at first. The more you practice, the easier it becomes. With time, vulnerability will become your greatest source of strength.

Thinking for yourself is an ongoing practice. It's not something that happens overnight. It requires patience, consistency, and a commitment to your own personal growth. Every day presents an opportunity to practice speaking your truth, whether it's in your personal relationships, at work, or in public spaces.

Start small. Speak your mind in conversations with friends, share your ideas in meetings, and don't shy away from challenging the norm when it feels right. The more you practice speaking out loud, the more natural it will feel.
Remember, your voice matters. Your thoughts and ideas have value. The world needs the uniqueness that only you can bring.

While the courage to think for yourself comes from within, surrounding yourself with people who support your independence is crucial. Seek out communities, mentors, and friends who encourage you to speak your truth, even when it feels uncomfortable. These supportive voices will help you build the confidence to keep speaking up and thinking freely.

The people around you can either amplify or diminish your courage to think for yourself. Surrounding yourself with like-minded individuals who value authenticity and independent thinking will help you stay grounded in your power.

Thinking for yourself and speaking out loud brings a sense of freedom. Freedom from the constraints of societal expectations, freedom from self-doubt, and freedom from living in someone else's shadow. When you step into your own power, you no longer feel the need to apologise for your thoughts or second-guess your opinions. You become the author of your own story, and that is an empowering place to be.

Authenticity is your birthright. The more you embrace it, the more your inner strength grows, and the more you'll find yourself drawn to the people and opportunities that truly align with your values.

Own Your Voice. I have always spoken my mind. There is nothing wrong with having a voice, especially if it is going to help people.

The courage to think for yourself and speak your truth is one of the most empowering decisions you can make. It's an act of self-love and respect. It requires you to trust in your own voice, challenge societal norms, and be comfortable with vulnerability. As you continue this journey of self-expression, you will inspire others to do the same, creating a ripple effect of courage, authenticity, and empowerment.

The world is waiting for your voice. Don't hold back, it will only lead to regrets.

66

'THINK LIKE A BOSS'

Unknown

Chapter 11

Own your power!...

I want to inspire you to take charge of your life, embrace leadership, and cultivate the mindset of someone who is in control of their success.

It is all in the power of your mindset. Thinking like a boss isn't just about having a title or owning a business, it's about how you carry yourself, how you make decisions, and how you approach challenges. I believe that a "boss" mindset is rooted in self-confidence, ownership, and vision. It's about thinking strategically, leading yourself and others, and taking responsibility for your actions.

Sounds exciting and scary right. I didn't know where to begin, but I knew I had a vision, determination, that I was consistent, persistent and that I could overcome challenges. I just needed that self-confidence to really go for it.

I have a silent confidence. I was often told that I have great leadership qualities, but my lack of confidence was holding me back. I am still working on that and getting uncomfortable by doing things that will build my confidence daily.

Anyone can adopt a "boss" mindset, regardless of their current situation, job, or stage in life. It's a way of thinking that empowers you to take control and create your own path. You are the CEO of your life.

Take ownership of your life and decisions. A boss doesn't blame circumstances or other people for their outcomes, they take full responsibility for their choices. This is the essence of empowerment. I want to help you shift from a mindset of "I can't" or "I'm not capable" to "I am the creator of my own destiny." Let's stop playing the victim and start asking yourself, what can I do right now to move forward?

I hope that I can inspire you to take ownership of both your successes and failures, because each experience is an opportunity to learn. Every time you fall, get back up and keep moving forward.

Create confidence in your vision. Thinking like a boss starts with having a clear vision of where you want to go. Clarity is so important. A boss knows where they are heading and stays focused, even when distractions or challenges arise.
Set big, bold goals and break them down into actionable steps.
Visualise your success. Imagine yourself as confident, competent, and powerful leaders of your own life. Trust in your vision, even when others may not see it yet.

I did this by visualising being a best selling Author...You never know.

I never thought that my favourite author would be helping me write my books and be so supportive along the way. Your visions can come true.

Bosses are problem-solvers, not complainers. When faced with challenges, a boss mindset focuses on solutions instead of dwelling on obstacles. You need to take charge of your life by approaching every difficulty as an opportunity for growth.

Ask yourself, how can I turn this situation into an advantage? or what's the lesson in this?

Every problem that you face can be a stepping stone towards greater success, if you decide to adopt a proactive, solution-oriented attitude.

Lead with self-belief. Thinking like a boss requires a strong sense of self-belief. It's about knowing your worth and not being afraid to show up as your true self. When you believe in your own abilities, others will naturally follow.

Silence your inner critic and replace negative self-talk with affirmations of power and potential. Embrace your unique strengths and use them to your advantage.

Confidence isn't arrogance. It's a deep, unwavering belief in your own value and abilities.

Take smart risks. A boss knows that progress comes from taking calculated risks. Embrace the idea that growth happens outside of your comfort zones. Thinking like a boss means being willing to step into the unknown, make bold moves, and trust the process.

Take measured risks in your personal or professional lives, whether it's asking for a promotion, starting a side hustle, or pursuing a new passion. You have nothing to lose. Not every risk will lead to success, but each experience is a valuable lesson.

Be disciplined and consistent. One of the most powerful traits of a boss is consistency. Success doesn't happen overnight. It's built through daily habits, discipline, and focus. Small, consistent actions accumulate into big results. 6 months of laser focused hard work, and dedication can set you 5 years ahead of the rest.

Surround yourself with the right people. You might lose a lot of people during this journey, but you will also meet the right people along the way. A boss knows that they can't achieve success alone. Building a strong network of supportive, like-minded individuals is essential. Seek out mentors, peers, and collaborators who inspire and challenge you.

Invest time in building relationships that nurture your goals. Do not be afraid to distance yourself from negativity or people who drain your energy. You need to stay confident and focused.

Find and build a community that celebrates your successes and pushes you to go further. The people that I thought would support me in my ventures, were the ones that went radio silent. It can be hurtful, but we need to keep going until we find our tribe.

Focus on the big picture! Bosses don't get bogged down by every setback. They keep their eyes on the long-term vision. Setbacks are temporary, but your vision and goals are what truly matter. I write this while I am going through a huge setback in my life. In fact, writing this book is distracting me from the stress and worry that I am under. I still want to help you all during my lows because it will make me feel more gratitude and feel grounded knowing that this is only temporary and things ARE going to get better. Revisit your goals and remind yourself why you are working towards them. Find purpose in the daily grind and use setbacks as motivation to keep pushing forward.

Remember, thinking like a boss is not about power over others. It's about power over yourself. It's about stepping into your own potential, owning your decisions, and leading your life with confidence and integrity. I encourage you to adopt this mindset today, take charge of your path, and lead your dreams with purpose.

Own your boss mindset!

66

'THE MOST BEAUTIFUL
WOMAN IS NOT AFRAID TO
BE HERSELF'

Unknown

———————————————————

Chapter 12

I like who I am becoming...A lot!

"The most beautiful woman is not the one who is admired from afar; she is the one who is unapologetically herself and owns her authenticity." — Unknown

It has taken me a very long time to truly be and love myself, and I still have my moments.

In a world that constantly tells us who we should be, what we should look like, and how we should act, the most beautiful woman is the one who is not afraid to be herself. She doesn't conform to society's expectations or wear a mask to fit in. Instead, she embraces her uniqueness, her flaws, and her power. She knows that true beauty comes from within, and it is only when she fully accepts and loves herself that she shines the brightest.

Too often, we are taught to hide parts of ourselves to be accepted. We learn to wear the "right" clothes, speak in a certain way, or even adjust our personalities to fit in with others. But the most beautiful woman knows that hiding who she is only dims her light.

True beauty is found in the courage to be authentic,

unapologetic and fearless. When you embrace your true self, you stop pretending to be someone you're not. You stop seeking approval from others because you've already made peace with who you are. The more authentic you are, the more beautiful you become.

There's a powerful magnetism that comes with being authentic. People are drawn to those who are real because authenticity is rare. When you let go of trying to please others or fit into preconceived molds, you unlock your unique brilliance. Your true beauty shines through because it comes from a place of self-love and confidence.

Perfection is an illusion, and the more we chase it, the more we lose ourselves. The most beautiful woman is not afraid to let go of the need to be perfect. She understands that perfection is not only unattainable but also unnecessary.

Our flaws, mistakes, and imperfections are what make us human, and they are part of what makes us beautiful. The woman who is not afraid to be herself embraces her imperfections. She understands that beauty is found in the moments of vulnerability, in the scars that tell the story of her strength, and in the ways, she continues to grow and evolve.

When you let go of the pressure to be perfect, you free yourself to fully experience life and be your true self. You no longer hold yourself to impossible standards, and you begin to realise that your authenticity is your perfection. The most beautiful woman knows this, and she walks through the world with confidence, knowing that she is enough, just as she is.

Self-acceptance is the foundation of not being afraid to be yourself. The most beautiful woman is the one who accepts herself fully, body, mind, and soul. She no longer criticises or compares herself to others. She understands that her worth is not determined by her appearance, her job title, or the opinions of others.

When you accept yourself, you release the need for validation from the outside world. You stop measuring your worth against the standards set by society, and instead, you measure it by the way you feel about yourself. The beauty of self-acceptance is that it allows you to stand tall, proud of who you are, and to move through life with confidence.

It's essential to embrace the truth that no one else can be you, and that is what makes you special. The most beautiful woman is the one who looks in the mirror and sees her value without needing anyone else's approval. She is not afraid to be herself because she understands that she is enough.

There is no one else like you in the world. You are a unique combination of experiences, perspectives, and qualities that cannot be replicated by anyone else. The most beautiful woman is the one who embraces this uniqueness. She does not try to fit into a box or compare herself to others because she understands that her individuality is her greatest asset.

The beauty of being yourself is that you get to define what beauty means to you. You get to create your own rules and live by your own standards. The most beautiful woman embraces the fact that she is different, and she knows that this difference is what sets her apart from the crowd.

When you embrace your uniqueness, you stop worrying about what others think of you. You stop hiding the parts of yourself that make you different. Instead, you celebrate those differences and wear them proudly. This is the essence of true beauty, owning who you are, without fear or hesitation. The most beautiful woman is not afraid to be herself because she has released the fear of judgment. She understands that no matter what she does, someone will always have an opinion, but she doesn't let that control her. Judgment can be one of the most paralysing fears. We worry about what others will think of our appearance, our decisions, or our choices. But when you stop worrying about the judgments of others, you reclaim your power. The most beautiful woman knows that the only opinion that matters is her own. She doesn't let the judgments or expectations of others dictate her actions or her sense of self-worth.

She understands that everyone has their own journey, and their opinions are just reflections of their experiences, not truths about her. She is guided by her own values, her own vision, and her own sense of self.

The most beautiful woman is not afraid to live her life with purpose and passion. She knows that beauty is not just about how she looks, it's about how she lives. When you are passionate about your life, your goals, and your dreams, you radiate an energy that draws others to you.

When you live authentically, you create a life that feels meaningful and fulfilling. The most beautiful woman doesn't shrink from her passions. She pursues them fearlessly and with enthusiasm. Whether she's building a career, nurturing relationships, or pursuing her dreams, she does so with purpose, and it's that inner drive and fire that makes her truly beautiful.

The most beautiful woman doesn't just keep her authenticity to herself, she inspires others to do the same. When you are not afraid to be yourself, you give permission to others to do the same. Your courage to embrace your true self is contagious.

By living authentically, you become a role model for others

to follow. You show them that it's okay to be different, to stand out, and to live a life true to who they are. The most beautiful woman creates a ripple effect of empowerment, inspiring other women to embrace their own uniqueness and live fearlessly.

You Are the Most Beautiful When You Are Yourself

When you embrace your authenticity, your uniqueness, and your imperfections, you become confident in knowing your worth, and don't fear judgment, and you also start to live with purpose and passion.

When you are not afraid to be yourself, you unlock your inner beauty, and you radiate it in every area of your life. True beauty comes from within, and it is only when you fully accept and embrace who you are that you can step into your power and shine your light.

Don't be afraid to be yourself. Your authenticity is your greatest beauty, and the world needs you to shine.
So, stop worrying about being judged and go and live your best life!

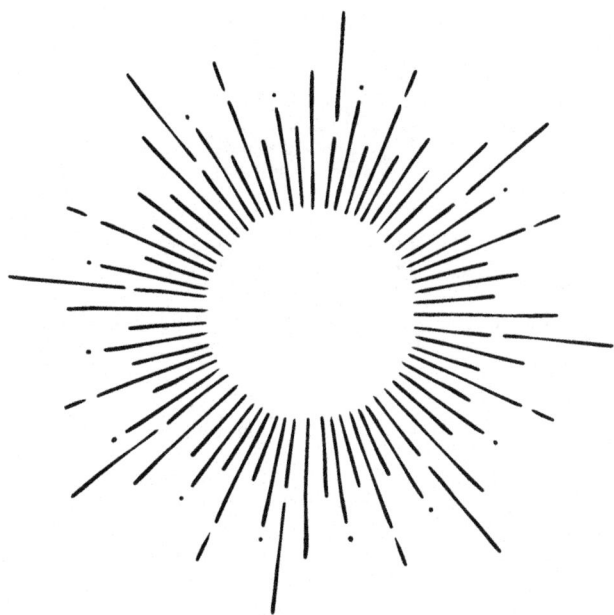

66

'I HAVE NO LIMITS AS TO WHAT I CAN ACHIEVE'

Anika Patel

Chapter 13

Break that glass ceiling...

Another one for the ladies….
Break free from limitations. Limitations from society, from family, from friends, from colleagues and from YOURSELF!

Throughout history, women have been told what they can or cannot do. These messages came in the form of societal expectations, limiting roles, or even direct discouragement. But in every generation, women have broken through barriers, rewriting the narrative of what is possible. As women, we have inherited a rich legacy of resilience, determination, and strength, and yet, the most powerful truth remains there is no limit to what we can accomplish.

We need to instill the power of belief in ourselves. The first step that I took towards unlimited potential is belief. Belief in myself and my abilities is the fuel that propelled me forward, even when the road ahead seemed uncertain. When we shift our mindset from doubt to confidence, we start to view challenges not as obstacles, but as opportunities for growth.

Our minds are powerful. They can either uplift us or hold us back. The belief that we can achieve greatness transforms the way we approach life. When we see ourselves as empowered, we tap into the limitless reservoir of potential that resides within us.

Believing in yourself is not about arrogance, but about recognising your worth, talents, and abilities. Every woman has a unique set of skills and experiences that contribute to the greater good of the world. When we embrace these qualities, we open the door to endless possibilities.

Let us redefine success on our own terms! Too often, the definition of success has been shaped by a patriarchal society, where achievements are measured by rigid standards that do not always account for the diverse ways women contribute to the world. But we, as women, have the power to redefine success on our own terms.

Success is not a one-size-fits-all concept. For some, it might mean climbing to the top of a corporate ladder, while for others, it could mean building a nurturing family or running a successful creative business. Success is about finding fulfilment in the pursuit of our passions and living authentically.

To achieve success on our own terms, we must be willing to trust our instincts, challenge the norm, and create a path that aligns with our values and aspirations. When we stop measuring ourselves against someone else's yardstick, we free ourselves from unnecessary pressure and begin to make choices that lead to our personal growth and happiness.

We need to overcome external and internal barriers. While the world has made strides toward gender equality, there are still numerous obstacles that women face, both externally and internally. Externally, we may encounter biases, glass ceilings, or systemic barriers that try to limit our progress. Internally, we may battle with self-doubt, fear of failure, or imposter syndrome. These challenges can sometimes feel overwhelming, but they are not unstoppable.

The key to overcoming external barriers is to recognise our power and pursue what we want, regardless of the obstacles in our way. History is full of women who defied the odds, including trailblazers like poets, writers, scientists, and so on. These women achieved greatness not because they had an easy path, but because they refused to let external limitations define their journey.

Internally, it's important to acknowledge our fears and self-doubts but not let them control us. Instead of focusing on what might go wrong, focus on what can go right. Affirmations, mentorship, and surrounding yourself with supportive people can help dismantle the internal barriers that keep you from reaching your fullest potential.

The power of community and support is magical. Women are stronger when we uplift and support one another. In a world that sometimes encourages competition, it's crucial to embrace collaboration. When we share knowledge, resources, and experiences with one another, we create a foundation of empowerment that can help us all rise.

As we succeed individually, we inspire others to believe that they, too, can achieve greatness. By championing one another and celebrating each other's victories, we create a ripple effect of empowerment that extends far beyond ourselves. Whether it's through coaching, partnerships, or community-building, the power of collective support cannot be underestimated.

Break through limiting beliefs. A huge barrier to success for many women is the limiting beliefs we carry with us, often subconsciously. These beliefs are formed from childhood messages, societal conditioning, or past experiences that tell us we are not enough. Yet these beliefs are not facts, they are just stories we've been taught to believe.

To break free from these limiting beliefs, we must first identify them. What are the thoughts or stories that have held you back? Are they true, or have they simply been ingrained in you over time? Once we question these beliefs, we can begin to replace them with empowering thoughts that support our growth and success.

I use affirmations like "I am worthy of success," "I have the power to achieve my goals," and "My potential is limitless" which helps to shift my mindset and dismantle the negative beliefs that have held me back. Every time we choose to believe in our abilities and our worth, we take another step toward breaking free from limitations.

The key to manifesting your dreams is taking action. Having a vision is crucial, but without action, that vision remains just a dream. Women who accomplish incredible things are not only dreamers but doers. They take bold steps toward their goals, no matter how small or large. Whether it's starting a project, or simply learning something new, every action counts.

The process of action is where growth happens. It's where we learn from our mistakes, refine our skills, and build resilience. Even when we face setbacks, taking action teaches us how to adapt and move forward. Progress is made one step at a time, and every step brings us closer to realising our potential.

I want you to feel empowered to achieve the impossible There are no limits to what women can accomplish when we embrace our power, trust our abilities, and take action. We are not bound by the limitation's that others have tried to impose on us. Instead, we have the power to redefine success, break through barriers, and achieve anything we set our minds to.

The world is waiting for us to step into our full potential, and there is nothing stopping us but the limits we place on ourselves. So, rise with confidence, chase your dreams without hesitation, and remember there is no limit to what we, as women, can accomplish. The world needs our brilliance, our strength, and our unwavering belief in the possibility of greatness.

66

'YOU ARE THE ONLY ONE
WHO LIMITS YOUR
GREATNESS'

Unknown

Chapter 14

The invisible chains that we create...

The only limits that exist are the ones you place on yourself." — Unknown

We live in a world that constantly pushes us to strive for more, to reach for greater heights, and to become the best version of ourselves. And yet, so many of us remain trapped in self-imposed limits that hold us back from achieving our fullest potential. The truth is that the only person who can truly limit your greatness is you. I used to hold myself back a lot! I let the opinions of others hold myself back to. To this day, when I want to do something new in life that I know will be good for my well-being, my life and serve my highest good, I still get worried to take that step. I still feel worried that someone will try to hold me back with their negative words. I silently move forward though, and I encourage you to do the same.

We unknowingly place limits on ourselves. These limitations hinder our growth, I want to empower you on how to break free from these mental barriers to unlock the boundless potential within.

How I have broken free from the mental barriers that I placed on myself

From the moment we are born, we begin to internalise messages from the world around us. These messages come from our families, schools, society, and the media. We are told what we can and can't do, what is "realistic," and what we "should" aim for in life.

These external influences often shaped my self-perception and formed the foundation of my beliefs about what was possible. Over time, these external messages became internalised, forming invisible chains that held me back. I started to believe that I am too old, too young, too inexperienced, or not qualified to achieve my dreams.

These limitations weren't truths, they were simply beliefs. And they were beliefs that I had the power to challenge and change.

The stories that I told myself

The first step in overcoming self-imposed limits is recognising the stories we tell ourselves. These stories shape our reality, and too often, they are based on fear, doubt, or past failures rather than our true potential.

I used to tell myself:

- "I'm not good enough to pursue that career."
- "I'll never be able to lose the weight or get healthy."
- "I don't have the time, money, or resources to start my dream project."

These thoughts may feel true, but they are only stories that I told myself.

They are the mental scripts that I used to write about my life based on my current circumstances, past experiences, or what others had told me. To step into your greatness, you must change the script. Challenge these stories. I asked myself: "Is this really true? Is this belief serving me, or is it holding me back?"

The power of belief in my own potential
At the core of every limit is the belief that you are not enough or that you are not capable. But here's the truth, you were born with everything you need to succeed. Your potential is limitless, and the only thing standing between you and your dreams is the belief that you cannot achieve them. Believing in your potential is the most powerful force you can harness. When you believe in yourself, you begin to see opportunities where others see obstacles. You take risks. You step outside of your comfort zone. You embrace challenges because you know they are part of the process of growth and expansion. Belief in yourself is the foundation upon which greatness is built. If you don't believe you can do something, then you've already created a limit for yourself. But when you believe, you begin to unlock the doors to possibilities that once seemed out of reach.

One of the biggest limitations that I placed on myself is the fear of failure. I feared that if I try and fail, I will prove to myself and others that I am not capable. This fear, however, is rooted in the illusion that failure means something permanent or final.

Failure is simply feedback. It's not an end. It's part of the journey. Every great achiever, from inventors to entrepreneurs to athletes, have failed countless times before achieving success. The difference is that they didn't let failure define them. Instead, they used it as a stepping stone to get closer to their goal.

Fear, when seen through this lens, becomes less of an obstacle and more of an opportunity for growth. Instead of avoiding it, embrace it. Know that on the other side of fear lies the success, growth, and self-empowerment you're seeking.

Your comfort zone is your prison. Our comfort zone is where we feel safe and secure, but it is also where growth stagnates. When you stay in the familiar, when you avoid taking risks or challenging yourself, you are essentially placing a limit on your greatness.

Growth only happens when you step outside your comfort zone and take action that scares you a little bit. Whether it's speaking up in a meeting, starting a business, asking for a promotion, or pursuing a new skill, the moments of discomfort are often the very moments that signal growth.

To break free from the prison of your comfort zone, you must make the decision to stretch yourself. Start with small, manageable steps, and with each one, you'll build the confidence to take bigger risks. The more you step out, the more you'll realise that the limits you once placed on yourself were never real, they were just the stories you told yourself to stay comfortable.

You are not defined by your past. One of the biggest barriers to greatness is the belief that your past defines your future. If you've failed before, struggled with challenges, or made mistakes, you may believe that these experiences limit your potential.

But your past does not define you. It is simply a chapter in your story. What matters is the decision you make today to move forward. Your past mistakes do not dictate your future success. The lessons you've learned from them are the stepping stones towards your greatness.

Don't let the mistakes or failures of yesterday keep you stuck. You have the power to reinvent yourself, to start fresh, and to create a future that reflects your true potential. The past is a teacher, not a prison.

Break free from self-imposed limits. The most empowering realisation is that you have the ability to break free from the limits you've placed on yourself. You are the only one with the power to lift the chains that bind you.

I did this, by:

1. Identifying my limits: What are the beliefs, fears, and stories that held me back? I wrote them down and examined them closely.

2. Challenging these limits: I asked myself if these beliefs were based on facts or assumptions. Are they serving my growth, or are they keeping me stuck?

3. Rewriting my story: I begin to rewrite the narrative of my life. I focused on my strengths, my potential, and the limitless possibilities before me.

4. Taking action: I began to take small steps towards my dreams, even if they felt uncomfortable. Every step forward, no matter how small, is a victory.

Remember, you are the creator of your own reality. The only limits that exist are the ones you place on yourself. It's time to break those limits and step into the greatness that has always been waiting for you. YOU ARE LIMITLESS.

Your greatness is not determined by your circumstances, your past, or the opinions of others. It is determined by your belief in yourself and your willingness to push beyond the limits you've imposed on your own potential. The only thing standing in your way is you. But once you break free from those self-imposed limits, you'll discover a world of endless possibilities and opportunities. It's time to remove the chains, step into your power, and embrace the limitless potential within you.

66

'I AM LIMITLESS'

Unknown

———————————————————

Chapter 15

Your potential is endless!...

So, what does it mean to be limitless?

Being limitless is the ability to decide to be and do anything that is aligned in your heart and in harmony with you and the world for your highest good. You do not need to get approval from anyone to do so.

Therefore, we all have the power to be and feel limitless.
The only person that can really hold you back is yourself, not anyone else. Not the opinions of others or their words.
A persons own limiting beliefs should never hold you back from your dreams. Another person's own fear and insecurities should not stop you from succeeding in what you want to do in life.

I was told by many people that I will never be able to write and publish a book. But here I am writing my second one. Did I let those words stop me? No, it made me try harder because I wanted to help people and share my experiences and life lessons, in the hope that it may inspire others.

When we know ourselves and believe in what we are capable of, there is nothing that can stop us from going for what we want in life.

When we stop listening to the opinions of others and do what is right for ourselves and our life, we will automatically feel much happier.

Go for your dreams and do not let anyone ever hold you back or stop you from finding your purpose. When you find your purpose in life, you reach a place of contentment and fulfilment.

I have always followed my dreams and done things that I have set my mind to, or at least tried, even if it may not work out. I put my 100% effort into achieving my goals, and if I succeed then great! If not, then that's fine too. At least I will not have any regrets. Even when I have had doubts, and not completely believed in myself, I have pushed through! Even when people have told me that I can't and never will be able to achieve my goals, I didn't listen. I continued anyway. I have been told 'NO, you can't', 'you will never' many times, but I have never let it stop me.

You have one life! Make the most of it. Do what you want without fearing the outcome. Believe in yourself and be confident in your abilities – AND BE LIMITLESS!

Because you are! And you can do anything that you put your mind to. If you still think that you can't, I want you to know that I believe in you!

So, step back into your power and take control of your life, instead of putting it into the hands of others.

It will set you free!

Thank You

Thank you all so much for reading the second part of my mini book series. I hope that you have enjoyed it and found it useful, and most of all I hope that it has encouraged and motivated you to believe in yourself more.

I hope that by me sharing my voice and experiences, it has inspired you to really trust in yourself and know that you can turn your life around with these small mindset shifts and practices. Anything is possible if you really believe in it, and make it happen.

For more empowering content, please follow me on my Instagram page:

@Empowering_the_mind

I will see you there!...

Before I Forget!

Please take photos of yourself reading my book and post them on your Instagram stories, tagging me on:

@Empowering_the_mind

Feel free to also post your favourite quotes or favourite parts of the book to your Instagram stories too and tag me on:

@Empowering_the_mind

And, lastly...

I have shared some empowering affirmations on the next couple of pages to help you tap into your limitless potential.

Repeat these affirmations daily to align yourself with a mindset of empowerment and limitless possibility!

LIMITLESS EMPOWERMENT

AFFIRMATIONS

I am worthy of all the abundance that life has to offer.

Every challenge I face is an opportunity for growth and strength.

I trust in my abilities and my inner wisdom to guide me.

I am capable of achieving anything I set my mind to.

I release all doubts and embrace my true power.

I am a magnet for success, prosperity, and positivity.

My thoughts create my reality, and I choose to think big.

I am fearless in the pursuit of my dreams and goals.

I am constantly evolving into the best version of myself.

The universe supports me in all my endeavors.

I am deserving of love, respect, and success.

Every day, I am becoming more confident and empowered.

I radiate confidence, vitality, and joy.

I am limitless, unstoppable, and capable of greatness.

I trust the process and surrender to the flow of life.

66

'I AM
LIMITLESS IN THE PERSUIT
OF WHAT I DESIRE'

Unknown

_____

Further Reading

Every effort has been made to reference and credit the books and quote sources correctly. But, if any have been overlooked by mistake or incorrectly referenced, please contact the author.

I. Hay, Louise L., You Can Heal Your Life (Hay House, 1999)

II. Dyer, Wayne W., The Power of Intention: Change the Way You Look At Things And The Things You Look At Will Change: Learning to Co-Create Your World Your Way (Hay House 2004)

Quote Credits

Chapter 1:
No One Can Make You Feel Inferior Without Your Consent. Stoic Quotes.
https://stoicquotes.com/no-one-can-make-you-feel-inferior/
accessed March 2025

Chapter 8:
She remembered who she was and the game changed.
https://www.goodreads.com/author/quotes/16169716.Lalah
_Delia
Accessed March 2025

Quote Credits Continued...

Chapter 10:

The most courageous act is still to think for yourself. Aloud. Quote.
https://www.goodreads.com/quotes/75485-the-most-courageous-act-is-still-to-think-for-yourself
Accessed March 2025

About Me

My name is Anika Patel and I am from London. My dream and vision is to help you empower your mind, and really help you start to realise what you are capable of when you step into your power, take control of your life and believe in yourself. I decided to do this by sharing my voice and my journey through my love of writing.

Embarking on my own self-love and healing journey has really started to transform my life in such a positive way, and I have learnt so much along the way, and still am. I have been using my social media platforms and podcast to share my knowledge, experience and tips on everything I have learnt on all things self-love, self-worth, self-empowerment and so much more, and I want to continue to help others to kickstart their self-love journeys and make positive changes to transform their lives too.

My aim is to inspire, empower, motivate and encourage every one of you to be the best version of yourselves that you can be, by empowering you to love yourselves from the inside out and unlock that limitless potential.

Printed in Great Britain
by Amazon

61129312R00070